ANIMAL OLYMPIANS

ANIMAL ≋
OLYMPIANS

THE FASTEST, STRONGEST, TOUGHEST, AND OTHER WILDLIFE CHAMPIONS

THANE MAYNARD

A Cincinnati Zoo Book
FRANKLIN WATTS
New York • Chicago • London • Toronto • Sydney

This book is dedicated to the MAE (Men Against the Elements),
who explored the Florida wilds with me back before the developers
paved over everything—Ray Coleman, Doug Blaze, Dave Boone,
Bob Medsger, Dean Whitehill, Dave Beede,
Ken Ward, and Craig Reisinger.
The older we get, the wilder we were.

Cover photographs copyright © Cincinnati Zoo/Ron Austing except: Indianapolis Zoo, top center;
Cincinnati Zoo, bottom left

Photographs copyright ©: Cincinnati Zoo/Ron Austing: pp. 2 left, 2 right, 3 center, 3 right, 6, 8, 10, 11, 12, 14 top, 15 bottom, 16, 17, 18, 19, 22 top, 25 top, 31, 32, 34 top, 42, 43 bottom, 49 right, 51 left, 52, 53 top left, 53 bottom, 54, 56, 61 bottom; Marine Mammal Images, Inc./Mark Conlin: 14 bottom, 46; Cincinnati Zoo/R. Scars: p. 22 bottom; Visuals Unlimited, Inc.: 25 bottom (C. P. Hickman), 26 (Walt Anderson), 37 (William J. Weber), 38 (Kjell B. Sandved); Cincinnati Zoo/Stan Rullman: pp. 28 top, 30 left; Cincinnati Zoo/Carl Hilker: p. 29; Cincinnati Zoo/Luther C. Goldman: p. 34 bottom; Innerspace Visions/Doug Perrine: p. 39; Cincinnati Zoo/Maslowski: p. 45; Indianapolis Zoo: pp. 2 center, 48; Cincinnati Zoo/Milan Busching: p. 58 left; all other photographs copyright © Cincinnati Zoo.

Library of Congress Cataloging-in-Publication Data

Maynard, Thane.
Animal olympians / Thane Maynard.
p.   cm.
"A Cincinnati Zoo book."
Includes bibliographical references and index.
ISBN 0-531-11159-8 (lib. bdg.)—ISBN 0-531-15715-6 (pbk.)
1. Animals—Miscellanea—Juvenile literature. [1. Animals—
—Miscellanea.] I. Title.
QL49.M485 1994
591—dc20   93-30769 CIP AC

CONTENTS

INTRODUCTION 7

GROWING UP WILD 9

THE LONGEST DRINK OF WATER 10

THE MOST DANGEROUS ANIMAL 12

RECORD-SETTING PREGNANCIES 13

THE OLYMPIC BUTTERFLY 17

THE STANDING LONG JUMP CHAMPION 19

BREATH-HOLDING FINALISTS 21

THE EARTH'S HEAVYWEIGHT DIGGING CHAMPION 24

ABLE TO LEAP TALL FENCES AT A SINGLE BOUND 27

SPEED CHAMPIONS 29

THE SPITTING CHAMPION 32

THE MOST FREQUENT FLYER 33

THE BIGGEST BITE IN THE SEA 35

AQUATIC GOLD MEDALISTS 37

HOVERCRAFT HUMMINGBIRDS 39

HEARTBREAKING RECORDS . . . RECORD-BREAKING HEARTS 41

THE SWIFTEST BIRD 44

THE FASTEST-GROWING ANIMAL ON EARTH 46

LONGEST-LIVING ANIMALS 47

THE BIG SLEEP 50

THE FASTEST WINGS IN THE SKY 52

SKYDIVING CHAMPION 54

ANIMAL WEIGHT LIFTERS 56

THE INSECT-EATING CHAMPIONS 57

SOARING TO OLYMPIC HEIGHTS 59

GLOSSARY 62

FURTHER READING 63

INDEX 64

INTRODUCTION

When most people think of the Olympics they imagine the every-four-years-events of summer and winter in which women and men run around in circles, swim up and down in big, chlorinated bathtubs, and slide down mountain tops with long, narrow boards strapped onto their shoes. But human olympic athletes can hardly imagine the competition they would face in the real Earth olympics.

There are dozens of animals that can outrun, outswim, out-climb, and generally outmaneuver us. They have to; it is essential in order for them to survive in the wild. But all these physical abilities are not the result of a few years of intensive training, as for human athletes. Animal olympians are on Mother Nature's training program.

All wild species of plants and animals are perfectly adapted to fit into the habitat where they live. That's why they are there. Evolution is a slow process, involving millions of years of give and take through which species change very slowly, one generation at a time. The result is the intricate, diverse web of life with which we share the Earth.

But even the quickest, strongest and trickiest animals in the world can't win in the extinction game without our help. Remember, it takes more than talk to help save wildlife and wild places. Join or volunteer with a local conservation group. Spend as much time as you can outdoors—hiking, canoeing, camping—and be sure to take along your binoculars so at least you'll have the eyesight of an animal olympian. With enough time in the field, you may develop your vision of what it takes to save the wild.

ELEPHANTS TAKE THE LONGEST TO MATURE OF ALL MAMMALS—EXCEPT HUMAN BEINGS.

GROWING UP WILD

In the world of human beings, not everybody grows up at the same rate. Some people are late bloomers, while others flourish early. This is true in the natural world as well; the time it takes different animals to grow up varies by species. It can be as little as twenty minutes in the case of some bacteria, or over a decade for humans, elephants, crocodiles, and many turtles.

Lots of animals, including most reptiles, grow throughout their lives. However, scientists generally measure "growing up" as the length of time it takes for a creature to reach sexual maturity, the stage when they can **reproduce**. Microorganisms—tiny life-forms—are fast growers, but not all of them are as fast as bacteria. For instance, the amoeba takes almost three hours before it reproduces—by splitting in two. Fruit flies take about two weeks to mature, and the smallest of rodents takes about a month. The rabbit, known for its ability to produce many offspring, must be about eight months old in order to reproduce.

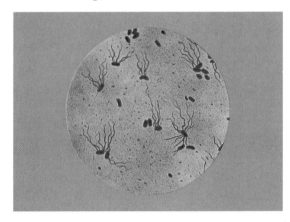

BACTERIA REACH MATURITY
IN RECORD TIME.

Many animals take more than a year to grow up. Wolves take about eighteen months, storks about four years, and bears between five and six years. People are slow to mature, taking around thirteen years generally, although parental care in some nations continues for years. Elephants are the slowest maturing of the mammals other than humans, taking about a decade to grow up.

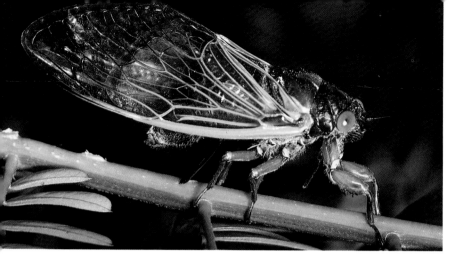

The world record for the animal that takes the longest to mature goes to, believe it or not, an insect. The seventeen-year cicada eventually emerges from below the ground by the billions. It is the slowest animal of all to reach reproductive age, patiently waiting underground for seventeen years until it climbs up, develops into a winged adult, and flies off in search of a mate. But when these cicadas do emerge from underground, they appear by the billions!

The important thing to remember is that whether quick or slow, there is no single best survival plan for animals. The forty million species of living things on earth have all worked out a special way of life that works for them. Personally, I'm glad people don't spend seventeen years underground like cicadas before they mature.

THE LONGEST DRINK OF WATER

Every living creature on Earth requires water in one way or another, but nothing beats the camel in its ability to drink. At a single sitting, a camel can drink enough water to half fill a bathtub. That's right, a camel can drink over 30 gallons (about 115 l) at one time. It would take a person one and a half hours of nonstop drinking from a water fountain (without spilling a drop) to drink that much. It takes a camel only ten minutes!

Camels drink so much because they live in the desert. Not all deserts are hot all the time—the Gobi Desert, home of the Bac-

CAMEL: CHAMPION DRINKER

trian camel, is freezing cold much of the year. However, all deserts are dry. So these animals fill up with as much as they can when they find a source of water.

The business end of a camel is the hump (or humps, as the case may be). But the humps are not water reservoirs. In fact, camels store fat in their humps. They draw on this reserve of energy—the fat—for use during dry times. They **metabolize** the fat to get needed moisture. Camels are said to be able to go for many miles and many days, sometimes up to a month, without food or water because of the energy supply they carry. Thousands of years before dune buggies or four-wheel-drive trucks, people were crossing deserts on camels—the original energy-efficient form of transportation.

THE MOST DANGEROUS ANIMAL

What is the world's most dangerous animal? Some people name the great white shark of the Pacific coast. Others suggest grizzly bears or tigers, or the crocodiles that live along the banks of the Nile and its tributaries and that, in fact, have eaten quite a few people through the history of human civilization. But the truth is, the most dangerous animal in the world, by far, is the mosquito.

Tiny mosquitoes might seem like just a nuisance, but they are a principal carrier or **vector** of diseases. With each bite, they can transmit a variety of germs that may cause malaria, yellow fever, or other illnesses. In most of the developed world these diseases are no longer major health risks; but in other areas, the annual death toll from mosquito-transmitted diseases is very high. Thus the mosquito remains the deadliest creature on Earth.

MOSQUITO: MOST DANGEROUS ANIMAL

The life history of the mosquito is fascinating. The female mosquito is the dangerous pest. Males are herbivores, or plant eaters, and are no threat to us at all. Female mosquitoes bite people and animals to sip their blood because it provides the extra protein they need. They are larger than males, and they carry and lay eggs.

All mosquitoes begin their lives in the water, as eggs that hatch out little wormlike larvae that float up to the water's surface to breathe. After two or three weeks in the water, the larvae transform into winged adults that fly off in search of food and mates. When they attack human beings and drink blood, they're just doing their job—in order to survive. Over millions of years mosquitoes have become perfectly adapted for this work. And we use all the defenses we have developed to try to get them *(splat!)* before they get us.

RECORD-SETTING PREGNANCIES

Nearly all 4,200 species of mammals give birth to live young. Except for the duck-billed platypus and the echidna, who lay eggs, all mammals have a **gestation period** during which they carry their babies inside the womb. However, the length of their pregnancies covers a huge range. The Asian elephant holds the record for the longest gestation, about two years, after which a 200-or-more-pound (90 kg) baby elephant is born. But that's not the biggest baby—even though it takes the longest to be produced. The blue whale is pregnant for about a year and the baby whale is about 23 feet (7m) long at birth and can weigh over 4,000 pounds (1,800 kg)!

On the other end of the scale are the **marsupials**, such as kangaroos and koalas, who all have extremely immature babies that find their way by instinct into their mother's pouch at birth.

ASIAN ELEPHANT: LONGEST GESTATION

BLUE WHALE WITH CALF: LARGEST BABY

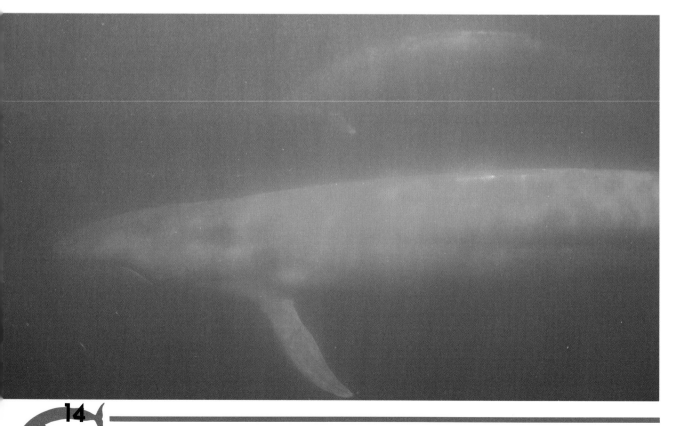

The opossum, another marsupial, has the shortest pregnancy of all. The babies are born after only a ten- to twelve-day gestation. They are about the size of jelly beans when they first emerge, but then they spend a few months in their mother's pouch before they venture out on their own.

The animal olympian with the tallest baby is the giraffe. Its young can be 6 feet (1.8m) tall at birth. The mother stands up to deliver it, and the youngster is born feetfirst and stands up shortly

GIRAFFE WITH OFFSPRING: TALLEST BABIES

after birth. Having a 6-foot-tall baby seems extraordinary, but since the giraffe is the tallest animal in the world, a shorter newborn wouldn't be able to reach its standing mother to nurse. And if it weren't born feetfirst, the baby might fall from 6 feet up, right onto its head.

In some bat species the babies literally take matters into their own hands, and feet. Bats live much of their lives upside down, and this means the young have to move upward to be born. So, the babies seem to deliver themselves. They start to emerge, and when the head and shoulders are free, they instinctively grab onto the mother's belly fur and pull themselves out of the womb. Then, still attached by the umbilical cord, they climb up to be suckled by the mother. In some species the mother bats may be fed by other bats, but after a day or two they are out flying about with their newborns hanging on for dear life.

BAT WITH BABY: MOST UNUSUAL BIRTH

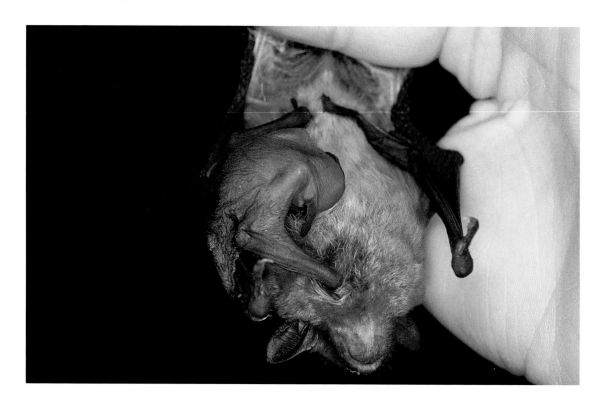

THE OLYMPIC BUTTERFLY

If you have ever been out on a fall day and noticed a great number of beautiful orange-and-black monarch butterflies, you have seen one of nature's tiny record breakers. Monarchs are, without competition, the farthest traveling insect in the world. The reason you see so many in the fall is that, like many birds, these butterflies migrate to a warmer climate for the winter. If you'd like to see this **migration** in full swing, head out to an open field for a picnic on a nice day in October and face south. If you are lucky you may see dozens of monarchs on their yearly journey to Mexico.

MONARCH BUTTERFLY:
FARTHEST TRAVELING INSECT

Can you imagine a tiny animal, weighing about as much as a postage stamp, making it from North America and even from Canada all the way to the forests of southern Mexico? It is true. These butterflies travel great distances to wintering grounds in the state of Michoacán, Mexico. Scientists believe they can fly about 50 to 100 miles (80 to 160 km) a day. That's better than we could do by walking.

THE MONARCH'S WINTER HOME

It wasn't until the 1970s that the monarch's winter location was discovered by Norah and Fred Urquhart, a husband-and-wife team of **entomologists**. This led the World Wildlife Fund and the Mexican government to establish a national preserve so that the beautiful monarch butterfly will always have a winter home. Today, as for the last decade, teams of scientists are monitoring the migration of monarchs by "banding" them.

The word banding, however, is misleading. With birds, actual bands are placed around a leg, but butterflies have tiny adhesive stamps placed on their forewings. When the banded, or labeled, monarchs are recaptured or found dead along their route, the information about their movements is fed into a national computer data base that serves as a tool to improve understanding of the animal's behavior.

BANDING
A BUTTERFLY

Since most other insects in North America have relatively short adult life spans, they do not migrate south for the winter as the monarch does. Instead, they lay eggs in protected areas, perhaps underground or in a tree's bark, and the next generation hatches out in the spring.

THE STANDING LONG JUMP CHAMPION

Anybody who has lived with a free-roaming cat or dog certainly knows something about fleas. They are wingless, tiny parasites—just about 1/8 inch (3 mm) long—that live by drinking blood and are famous for their jumping ability. You may wonder why we can't ever seem to get rid of them entirely. Consider the fact that fossil-flea-remains two hundred million years old have been found in Australia, making fleas one of the oldest known

FLEA:
CHAMPION JUMPER

insects. Today there are more than a thousand known species of flea living all over the world. It seems that the fabulous flea is here to stay.

Fleas have a complicated life history for such tiny creatures. After the egg stage, they undergo a complete **metamorphosis** that lasts from two days to two weeks. In the larval stage, they become tiny, legless caterpillars that feed on dried blood and adult flea feces. Next they spin a cocoon for the pupal stage, and finally, they emerge—all at once and in great numbers—as adults. This explains how a family may go away on a vacation only to return to find a population explosion of fleas, even though no pets were left at home.

It is important not to think of fleas just as bad guys. They are the gold medalists in the standing long jump. While bullfrogs, rabbits, and mountain lions are all famous jumpers, sometimes leaping up to ten times their body length, lowly fleas can easily jump 4 feet (1.2 m). And since fleas are less than ⅛ inch long (3 mm), that means they can jump 384 times the length of their bodies. To match the flea's record, Carl Lewis, the human gold medalist in the long jump, would have to leap nearly half a mile—from a standing start! People can't do that even going 70 miles

BONE-HEADED TREE FROG: ANOTHER SKILLED JUMPER

per hour (110 kph) off a ski jump! The world record in the ski jump is only 636 feet (194 m).

So, the next time you try to catch an annoying flea on your pet's back, remember that you are not dealing with just a pest, but with a true animal olympian!

BREATH-HOLDING FINALISTS

How long do you think you can hold your breath? Most people can go only a minute or two without taking a breath, but some animals can last many times longer than that. Walruses have been known to stay underwater for thirty-eight minutes without a breath. Among mammals, whales are undoubtedly the record breakers. Some whales can hold their breath for an hour, even while swimming at a quick pace in the sea. To accomplish this, their heart rates slow down and their blood flow is shut off to everything except their vital organs.

WALRUS: A BREATH-HOLDING FINALIST

A WHALE—THE BREATH-HOLDING CHAMPION—COMING UP FOR AIR

Smaller animals have ingenious ways to manage underwater. Some spiders carry an air supply down with them in the form of a bubble. This allows them to stay underwater for hours. Lots of diving insects perform a similar trick by trapping air in hairlike scales on their abdomens. Later they absorb the air through the little tubes, or spiracles, with which they breathe. That's why you see diving beetles floating upside down on the surface of a pond. They actually breathe through their tails, not their mouths, so theirs is a life spent "bottoms up."

DIVING BEETLE

Some animals have exactly the opposite problem: instead of needing to hold their breath while underwater, they need to hold it when out of the water. For instance, starfish, which get air through simple filters when underwater, are unable to breathe while on land. This doesn't mean that they quickly suffocate, as do many fish. Actually, they may survive for as long as an hour out of the water, because they have adapted to life in tide pools, where water levels often change.

STARFISH: UNDERWATER BREATHER

It's important to remember that these animal olympians hold their breath while remaining active. Many species can go without breathing for extended periods of time while sleeping and, especially, during **hibernation**. Some northern frogs and turtles can survive an entire winter hibernating underwater, but that is an entirely different situation than simply holding their breath.

THE EARTH'S HEAVYWEIGHT DIGGING CHAMPION

Aardvark means "earth pig." We can tell why *earth* is part of the name: these 6-foot-long (1.8-m), over 100-pound (45-kg) creatures dig their way into the earth to escape any threat that comes along. In fact, faced with the possibility of becoming dinner for a lion or pack of African wild dogs, an aardvark can burrow into the earth so quickly it seems to disappear. Aardvarks have been reported to burrow completely underground in less than a minute.

But the *pig* part of the name is misleading. Aardvarks aren't pigs at all. The animals aren't even related. Aardvarks belong to the order of animals called Tubulidentata, named for their tubelike teeth. An aardvark's teeth are all in the back of its mouth, ten on each side. These teeth are very simple and lack the enamel coatings our teeth

AARDVARK: CHAMPION DIGGER

have. Aardvark teeth are **porous**, like most bones, which allows a blood supply to flow through them.

The aardvark's teeth work like molars to grind up their favorite food—termites. In Africa, the aardvark's native region, termites live underground or in mounds. The hungry aardvarks use their flexible 18-inch (46-cm) tongues to fish out the insects. If that fails, they use their strong claws to carve out a hole right in the side of the termite nest. This is not easy because termite mounds become nearly as hard as rock after baking in the African sun. The angry little insects storm out to attack, but aardvark skin is tough enough to resist termite bites. And their long eyelashes and nostril hairs provide enough protection so they can go right on eating. These hairs also keep soil out of their noses and eyes when they dig.

TERMITES—THE AARDVARK'S PREY—
EMERGING FROM A MOUND

A HUGE TERMITE MOUND IN AFRICA

Aardvarks spend daylight hours in underground burrows and come out to hunt at night. They have an acute sense of smell and oversized ears that provide excellent hearing. Each ear can move independently, to scoop up sound like a radar receiver, enabling them to hear termites moving underground.

Unfortunately, aardvarks may have to be added to the **endangered species** list. They are in trouble not because of predators, or hunters, but because of the loss of wild **habitat** in Africa.

ABLE TO LEAP TALL FENCES IN A SINGLE BOUND

The red kangaroo is a tough customer for zookeepers. It is the largest of the kangaroos, weighing over 150 pounds (68 kg), and easily able to jump a 6-foot (1.8-m) fence from a standing position. It can hop nearly 30 feet (9 m) in a single bound and reach speeds of up to 45 miles per hour (72 kph). These awesome abilities and some others make the red kangaroo a most interesting animal.

Kangaroos' amazing hopping **locomotion** is actually a very efficient style of animal transportation. Their hind legs work like springs to propel them forward, so that when they are moving with speed they don't even use their front legs. The tendons in the hind legs serve as the springs, giving the kangaroos their bouncy gait. When they land, the force of impact stretches the tendons, which then compress again and thrust the animal forward. As a result, a kangaroo can keep up a 25-mile-per-hour (40-kph) "trot" for some time.

Like all kangaroos, the red kangaroo is a marsupial; the young are nurtured in the mother's pouch. And what a pouch it is! The female red kangaroo, like other kangaroos, produces two types of milk, from two nipples next to each other inside the pouch. One breast feeds a tiny, newly born immature infant;

KANGAROO: HOPPING CHAMPION

KANGAROO NURSING A JOEY

while the second feeds a joey, a baby who has already left the pouch. The more mature offspring no longer needs the pouch's protection from the elements, but it returns many times a day for its mother's milk, which is 33 percent higher in protein and over 400 percent higher in fat than the milk provided for the younger animal.

The red kangaroo has special abilities that help it survive in the harsh environment of central and southern Australia. Unlike most mammals, female red kangaroos can vary their rate of reproduction according to the conditions in their environment. For example, they may speed up the development of a **fetus** if one youngster dies.

SPEED CHAMPIONS

It's probably no news to anyone that the cheetah is the sprinting champion of the world, with a record of 71.6 miles per hour (115.2 kph) for the 100-yard (91.4-m) dash. When hunting, cheetahs often get within 100 yards or so of their prey before charging, so this seems a fair test of how fast they can go. However, most scientists agree that the average top speed of a cheetah is closer

CHEETAH: SPRINTING CHAMPION

to 60 miles per hour (97 kph), which is still fast enough for them to catch their prey.

The second fastest in running events is thought to be the pronghorn antelope of the American West. It can maintain speeds of 50 miles per hour (80 kph), for over an hour and runs the quarter-mile at a pace of 60 miles per hour (96 kph). A racehorse runs about 48 miles per hour (77 kph) for the same distance. But before you decide a racehorse is slow, remember that a horse is a great deal heavier than an antelope, and usually isn't being chased by a mountain lion.

Now let's look at the speed records of the white-tailed deer, the grizzly bear, and the domestic cat. These animals run at the same peak speed—30 miles per hour (48 kph) for short distances. Human beings can run only 22 to 28 miles per hour (35–45 kph).

PRONGHORN ANTELOPE:
RUNNING FINALIST

DOMESTIC CAT:
SHORT-DISTANCE RUNNER

Not all animals run along the ground. The gray squirrel zips along tree branches at about 12 miles per hour (19 kph), and the marten, a skilled acrobatic predator, races through the treetops at the record-breaking rate of over 23 miles per hour (37 kph).

Some other creatures may surprise you with their speed records. The elephant can charge at 25 miles per hour (40 kph). And the black mamba, one of the most deadly of all African snakes, scoots along at 20 miles per hour (32 kph). The lowly chicken can run the 100-yard dash at 9 miles per hour (14 kph).

Are you wondering about the tortoise and the hare? Rabbits run at about 27 miles per hour (43 kph), while tortoises, such as the giant Galápagos tortoise, cover the turf at only 0.17 miles per hour (0.27 kph). The garden snail, creeping along at a "snail's pace," is almost six times slower than the tortoise. It reaches a top speed of 0.03 miles per hour (0.05 kph) only when agitated. It would take an excited snail about a day and a half to slither a single mile (1.6 km)!

GARDEN SNAIL: SLOW TRAVELER

THE SPITTING CHAMPION

Along with the ordinary abilities of running, swimming, or flying, some species have special skills—such as spitting. My vote for the gold medalist in this competition goes to the archerfish of tropical Asia. This 3- to 4-inch-long (8–10 cm) freshwater fish gets its name from its ability to shoot water at insects, knocking them out of the air. The little fish shoots spit "arrows" straight up—over 12 inches (30 cm)—through a special slot in the roof of its mouth. The slot acts like a rifle barrel when the fish curls its tongue up against it to spit. Once the stunned insect hits the water, the fish gobbles it up.

The archerfish's shooting skill is even more amazing when we remember that the fish is shooting from under the water. If you've ever looked up at something through the water, you know it's hard to tell a person from a diving board, much less the exact location of a flying insect.

ARCHERFISH:
SPITTING CHAMPION

ARCHERFISH SPITTING

Another champion spitter is the spitting cobra, one of the deadliest snakes in the world. This animal has a **venomous** bite, which it uses as an offensive weapon, to capture prey. And it also can spit its venom to protect itself from being killed. The cobra can spit for a distance of up to 13 feet (4 m). If the venom gets into a predator's eyes, it causes extreme pain, and may even cause permanent blindness. So the spitting cobra uses its spit as a defense, and its venomous bite as an offensive weapon.

THE MOST FREQUENT FLYER

Throughout much of the world, if you look skyward during the spring or fall you'll see birds migrating. Many ducks and geese fly south for the winter, but a little bird called the Arctic tern holds the world record for traveling the greatest distance. This seabird gets its name from the fact that it lives part of its life up near the North Pole, in the Arctic Circle. But it spends an equal amount of time down at the South Pole! The Arctic tern could be the original frequent flyer, as it covers over 20,000 miles (32,000 km) round-trip every year.

The terns fly this much in search of their food—the little creatures that live in the cold waters of the world's oceans. In order for food to be abundant, there has to be ample sunlight. Arctic terns, therefore, follow the sun and are probably exposed to more sunlight than any other creature. Of course, they don't fly all 20,000 miles in one stretch.

ARCTIC TERN:
FARTHEST ANNUAL MIGRATOR

Scientists aren't certain, but they believe that terns fly about 1,000 miles (1,600 km) per week during twenty weeks of the year. The terns spend the rest of their time in feeding, mating, nesting, and taking care of other bird business.

Of the 660 species of birds that nest in North America, about half migrate south for the winter. And about one quarter, or 175 species, fly all the way to the tropical rain forests in Central and South America. Migration still holds some mysteries, but we do know that changes in the length of the day and the amount of light are among the triggers that send birds on their way. The reason birds do all this flying is, of course, for food. This is why all the insect-eaters migrate while most seed-eaters, like cardinals

A LEAST TERN, THE SMALLEST OF THE TERN SPECIES, IN FLIGHT

and goldfinches, stick around during the winter. And that's why it's a good idea to get out and buy some sunflower seeds and thistle, because no matter what the weather is now, your bird feeder will be a busy place when fall arrives.

THE BIGGEST BITE IN THE SEA

Just because an animal has a big mouth doesn't necessarily mean it has a powerful bite. Look at some whales, for instance. Blue whales have the largest mouth in animal history, but they don't have any teeth. And since they dine mostly on tiny invertebrates called krill, they have never needed to develop much of a bite at all. It's not until you look closely at some of the smaller, toothed whales that you find a big bite. Orcas, or killer whales, prey on large marine mammals such as seals and sea lions and so, of course, need a mouth full of teeth and a strong bite. But even the orca doesn't have half the reputation for biting that the shark has.

ORCAS: STRONG BITERS

On Jacques Cousteau and *National Geographic* television specials, we see divers go down in cages to get close to sharks. In order to test the strength of the bite of these quick and silent predators, scientists place gauges inside smaller fish that they use to attract the sharks. Then, when a shark bites down on the fish, the scientists can learn about its bite without having to test it "first hand." Good thing too, because recent studies on the medium-size blue shark have shown it has a bite of nearly 8,000 pounds (3,600 kg) of pressure per square inch! In fact, in earlier tests scientists had to keep developing tougher and tougher bite-o-meters, because the sharks chomped right through both the fish and the gauge. For comparison, a human bite is up to 250 pounds (113 kg) of pressure per square inch.

Among living sharks, the gold medalist in the biting competition would be the great white shark, but the truly record-breaking shark biters would be the long-**extinct** prehistoric sharks. One of these giants was *Carcharodon megalodon*. This shark had hundreds of teeth that were 4½ inches (11.4 cm) long and 4½ inches wide at the base, in a mouth that opened 7 feet (2.1 m) across.

GREAT WHITE SHARK: CHAMPION BITER

AQUATIC GOLD MEDALISTS

When people think of swimming champions, they usually picture Olympic gold medalists. Actually, human beings are only average swimmers. There's no way we can keep up with animals that are built for swimming. Human bodies are designed to stand up straight and walk, so in the water, thousands of animals can swim circles around us. The speed record for a human swimmer is now held by Tom Jager of the United States, who swam the 50-meter freestyle in 19.05 seconds in 1990. That sounds good, but it is only 5 miles per hour (8 kph).

Animals are in another class entirely. Among the more than 25,000 species of fish are some incredibly fast swimmers. The common and tasty tuna has been clocked at over 65 miles per hour (105 kph). And at least a few birds are quick in the water too, including the Gentoo penguin, which can swim 23 miles per hour (37 kph) when chasing fish or fleeing from leopard seals.

TUNA: SPEED-SWIMMING FISH

GENTOO PENGUINS: SPEED-SWIMMING BIRDS

The top swimming champion is the sailfish. These creatures have been known to swim alongside ships traveling at the speed of 68 miles per hour (109 kph). And not just for a sprint either; they are said to be able to swim at that speed for miles. They can accomplish this feat because of their streamlined shape that lets them glide through the water. Also, they are incredibly strong, with a series of muscles and an enlarged vertical tail, or caudal fin. They are not built for delicate maneuvering through the coral reefs, but have powerful muscles for long-distance swimming in

SAILFISH: SWIMMING CHAMPION

open water. And sailfish have big appetites, so they need to swim fast and far to find enough fish for their daily needs.

Since water is around 800 times denser than air, aquatic animals are slower, on the average, than birds; just as submarines are generally a good deal slower than airplanes.

HOVERCRAFT HUMMINGBIRDS

If you've ever looked closely at hummingbirds in flight, you've seen incredible miniature flying machines. Hummingbirds are the smallest of birds, many species weighing in at less than a single ounce (28 g). They are also the only birds that can actually back up, or go in reverse, while flying. These traits are vital to the hummers since they spend the largest part of the daylight hours hovering in front of flowering plants. To do this, hummingbirds need amazing wings. Their wings can perform 80 to 90 beats per second—the fastest wingbeat of all birds. And their wings don't just beat up and down, like those of a goose or a blue jay. A hummingbird actually turns its wings in a figure-eight motion to get lift. The style is a little like rowing a boat; the rower turns the oar on the backstroke so as to reduce drag. This is the bird's flying technique: the wings perform a double downstroke, one when they beat forward and the second when they beat backward.

The reason for the hovering, of course, is to enable the hummers to drink nectar from flowers. They are the principal actors in "the birds and the bees" story since, while flitting from flower to flower to collect nectar, they also carry pollen back and forth.

Hummingbirds don't live just on nectar, they back away from the flowers every few seconds and gobble up many of the little fruit flies that the sweet flowers also attract. So, the hummingbird's diet is a complete, well-rounded one, including sugars (nectars) for energy, of which they need plenty, and protein (fruit flies) for muscle growth.

HUMMINGBIRD: FASTEST WINGBEAT AND FASTEST HEARTBEAT

Hummingbirds also have the fastest heartbeat in the world, over 1,000 beats per minute, in order to power this flying phenomenon. But even with all the effort of these many wingbeats and heartbeats, some species have been known to live for over ten years.

There are 225 species of hummingbirds, and they are found only in the Western Hemisphere. Although a few species range as far as North America, the majority inhabit the tropical forests of Central and South America.

HEARTBREAKING RECORDS...
RECORD-BREAKING HEARTS

When you consider all the work that an animal's heart must do—pumping blood every minute of its life—it is not surprising that the heart muscle is the strongest in the entire body. The nearly microscopic heart of a bee hummingbird beats nearly 525,600,000 times in its just one year of life. And our own human hearts beat over three billion times during our average life span of seventy years.

But not everybody's heart beats to the same drummer. A good general rule when you are thinking about heart rates is that the larger the animal, the slower its heart beats. Generally, this rule holds true for warm-blooded animals, but the activity level of the animal plays a role too. For example, an elephant's heart rate is 30 beats per minute at rest—about half of ours. A wolf's heart beats about 100 times a minute, while the heart rate of a bat, which needs plenty of energy in order to fly, may be nearly 700 beats per minute.

The size principle works in the bird world, where hummingbirds' hearts have a rate of 1,000 beats per minute; those of medium-size songbirds like the blue jay a rate of 400 per minute,

GRAY WOLF: HEART RATE OF 100 BEATS A MINUTE

and that of the giant ostrich, which doesn't fly, 60 to 65 beats per minute.

Part of the reason that warm-blooded animals have higher pulse rates is that their bodies work hard just to keep up their normal body temperatures. This is not the case for cold-blooded creatures, such as reptiles, whose heart rates vary according to the temperature around them. A frog has a heart rate of 20 beats per minute at 50 degrees Fahrenheit (10°C); the heart rate rises to 50 beats per minute at 90 degrees (32°C). So, with cold-blooded animals, you might say that atmosphere makes the heart beat faster!

OSTRICH: HEART RATE OF
60 TO 65 BEATS
A MINUTE

AMERICAN ALLIGATOR:
VARYING HEART RATE

THE SWIFTEST BIRD

Swifts may be the most appropriately named animal anywhere, since they are the fastest-flying birds in the world. But what about the peregrine falcon? It has been clocked at over 200 miles per hour (320 kph). However, that figure is a peregrine's speed in a steep dive, not its average airspeed.

There are seventy-seven species of swifts all of which have characteristically long, pointy wings and can perform incredible acrobatics in flight. They have many adaptations that make them able to fly so quickly, but most important are their huge flight muscles that provide power, and their aerodynamic wing design that allows maneuverability.

Swifts also have the longest primary feathers in proportion to their total length of any of the approximately 9,000 species of birds in the world. In addition, the tiny barbs and barbules, which zip the wing feathers together, are especially tightly knit on the swifts. They also have a special feather "vent" in front of their eyes to protect against the rushing air while in flight, and their streamlined, cigar-shaped body offers minimum resistance in flight. The narrow, swept-back wings provide maximum efficiency for sustained high-speed flight.

All these features make the swift a true creature of the air. In fact, swifts can eat and drink on the wing, snapping up insects in midair and sometimes scooping water into their mouths as they skim over the surface of a stream.

Swifts fly in tight group formations, often by the tens of thousands. Huge migrating flocks, 15 or 20 miles (24 or 32 km) in length, have been seen. Swifts dwell in all parts of the world except the Antarctic, and are called various names that refer to their amazing flight patterns. Germans sometimes refer to them as "sail birds," although swifts, in fact, are not able to actually soar like the buzzards and hawks. In Brazil swifts are called "rockets," an appropriate name since the South American spine-tailed swift is thought to be the fastest of all the species. These birds are often seen shooting through the jungle, much like missiles, in their never-ending search for insects.

Even our common chimney swift is quite an acrobat, and nests high in smokestacks. Hollow trees were used for centuries before our arrival, and chimney swifts still nest in them, but we notice them more when they live closer to us.

CHIMNEY SWIFTS: FASTEST FLYERS

THE FASTEST-GROWING ANIMAL ON EARTH

The story of the first two years of a baby blue's life is a whale of a tale! The blue whale grows from an embryo the size of a speck of dust to a 13-ton mass in less than two years! It spends the first eleven months of that period inside the mother blue whale, and the next ten months as an infant.

The huge baby is born underwater and is pushed up to the surface by the mother to take its first vital breath of air. Then each day the baby whale consumes an average of 150 gallons (nearly 570 l) of its mother's milk, which is 50 percent fat, and so among the richest of all natural foods. To enable the baby to drink so much, the mother whale has a special set of muscles that work as a kind of "self-milking" machine. They squeeze the milk from the mother's **mammary glands** into the mouth of the calf, in a flow like that of a garden hose. The baby blue grows 1.5 inches (3.8 cm) and gains 200 pounds (90 kg) every day.

BLUE WHALE: FASTEST-GROWING ANIMAL

Whales grow so quickly for a good reason. Like all marine mammals, they need to be strong and to build a layer of fatty insulation to withstand a life in the cold ocean waters. Plus, if they are to reach over 100 feet (30 m) in length, it's vital to get started with a growth spurt.

Other whales are smaller than the great blue whale, both at birth, and when full grown. But all of the more than ninety species of whales are born in the same way, that is, they usually emerge tail, or fluke, first. Since whales breathe air, a baby could drown if the birth process was slow and its head was under water for a long time. After birth, it's up to the mother to get the newborn up to the surface quickly to breathe.

LONGEST-LIVING ANIMALS

We sometimes hear that fast-moving, hard-driving people are destined to live shorter lives than those who are more relaxed. Well, it's hard to know if that's true for humans or not, since so many other factors affect our **longevity**. But for some animals, at least, the story seems to be true. Picture the life of the longest-living creature on this planet, the giant tortoise which can live over 150 years. It lives, literally, in slow motion, moving along at a very deliberate and very, very sleepy pace. A probable second in the long-living competition would be the quahog mollusk, one of the giant clams of the ocean floor. It lives 100 years, just "as happy as a clam."

For the elephant, there seems to be evidence that metabolism and activity levels affect longevity. The African elephant averages about thirty-five years of life, while the Asian elephant usually lives about forty years. Some scientists feel this is because the Asian elephant is a more "laid back" creature, better able to relax than its cousin. The African elephant seems much more nervous, and never stops swaying back and forth, even at rest.

GIANT TORTOISE: LONGEST LIVING ANIMAL

Other animals are remarkable in different ways. Most whales, such as the orca, blue, and fin live about ninety years. So can the sea anemone. Some cockatoos and parrots live over seventy years, while the ostrich, largest of all birds, may be around for sixty-two years. On the other end of the scale, some of the tiny hummingbird and shrew species survive only one year.

Naturally, most longevity records are from animals held in captivity. It is hard to monitor a creature in the wild over a period of years, except in long-term field studies such as Jane Goodall's on chimps or Dian Fossey's on mountain gorillas. And even these studies show the natural longevity of only one or two individuals. It is also impossible to know how long wild animals could survive in their natural habitat, since they are constantly threatened by predation, disease, and starvation.

SEA ANEMONE:
LONG-LIVING WATER CREATURE

SHREW:
SHORT-LIVED ANIMAL

THE BIG SLEEP

In the colder parts of the globe wintertime is especially tough for some wild animals. Food and shelter are hard to find. Many small creatures survive these lean months by hibernating. Oddly enough, only relatively small creatures are able to drop into a deep sleep, although it is a common misconception that bears also hibernate. The truth is that bears, badgers, and others *sleep* through the worst of the winter weather in a den or cave. However they are still using energy, at about the same rate as in a normal night's sleep. The bears can be awakened and will aggressively pursue their prey—or the unlucky human being who accidently disturbed their sleep.

True hibernation occurs only when there is a drastic decrease

GRIZZLY BEAR: WINTER SLEEPER

in an animal's metabolic rate and body function. Generally, hibernating animals pass the winter without food, living off body fat stored during the preceding summer and fall, and using only one-fiftieth or less of the energy they normally require to function. The largest animal to truly hibernate is the marmot, a western cousin of the groundhog.

In hibernation, the animal's body temperature drops from close to 100 degrees Fahrenheit (38°C) down to near the freezing point of 32 degrees (0°C). As a safety guard, most animals curl up in as tight a ball as possible, exposing as little surface area as they can to the cold. But during very cold spells, some hibernators temporarily wake up and move around in order to warm up a little and keep their body tissues from becoming frostbitten.

The level of dormancy some animals reach during hibernation is mind-boggling. The chipmunk can slow its metabolism so much that its normal respiration rate of 60 is reduced to only 2 or 3 breaths per minute, and its heartbeat slows from 200 to a mere 10 per minute. The European hedgehog's hibernation is less startling, with a temperature drop from 95 degrees Fahrenheit (35°C) to around 50 degrees (10°C), and a heart rate of 20 beats per minute.

HEDGEHOG: ANOTHER WINTER HIBERNATOR

CHIPMUNK: CHAMPION HIBERNATOR

THE FASTEST WINGS IN THE SKY

Hummingbirds get their name from the fact that they are noisy fliers, literally humming along at a quick 80 to 90 beats a second on the fastest wings in the bird world. But that record is nothing when compared to that of some smaller-winged insect fliers. The world's record for wingbeats actually belongs to the tiny midgefly, which flies at the speed of only about 1/2 mph (0.8 kph), but beats its wings 1,000 times a second.

Before we take a deeper look into the various speeds of insects, consider the way they fly. Bird wings are aerodynamically shaped for flight by being curved on the leading edge and tapered in the rear. Insects, however, have flat wings. And, they have two pairs of wings instead of just one. Since insect wings are flat, they are used much the way oars are used to row a boat. They beat down to provide lift and backward to gain thrust. In some species the wings are clapped together at the top of each rotation and then thrown apart. This motion creates high-pressure **turbulence** below the wings that propels the insect both forward and upward. The turbulence is also the cause of most of the buzzing sound produced by the wings. The faster the wing beats, the higher the pitch of the buzzing.

INSECTS HAVE TWO PAIRS OF FLAT WINGS; BIRDS HAVE A SINGLE PAIR OF CURVED WINGS.

Interestingly, many of the large-winged insects, such as butterflies, fly relatively fast, but beat their wings very slowly. Monarch butterflies beat their wings only 8 times a second in order to fly nearly 5 miles per hour (8 kph). But the housefly and honeybee beat their wings over 200 times a second to reach the same speed. And that terrible buzzing of the mosquito is created by its 600 wingbeats a second. Yet all that effort yields a land speed of less than a single mile per hour (1.6 kph).

Beetles may be the slowest-flying order of insects. With their armored shape, many species are heavy bodied in relation to their wing size and have a sluggish flight pattern. If you've ever caught a ladybug or firefly (both are beetles) in your hand, you know they are none too quick. Some large tropical beetle species are even slower, sometimes using so much energy to fly that they can stay aloft only a few seconds at a time.

By contrast, the fastest-flying insects ever tested are dragonflies, clocked at about 18 miles per hour (29 kph), and hornets, which break the tape at 14 miles per hour (23 kph).

LADYBUG: A SLOW FLYER

HONEYBEE:
OVER 200 WINGBEATS
A SECOND

DRAGONFLY:
FASTEST FLYING INSECT

SKYDIVING CHAMPION

You may have seen sky divers float to Earth after jumping from an airplane. But a peregrine falcon swooping down out of the sky—with no helmet, parachute, or special flight suit—looks like a dive-bomber. Peregrines may be the most phenomenal flying machines that have ever existed.

When diving after prey, the peregrines can easily reach a speed of 200 miles an hour (320 kph) and have even been clocked at 224 miles an hour (360 kph). The peregrine generally hunts from high in the sky and once it spots its prey—usually another bird—turns downward quickly to pursue it. After a few quick wing beats to start, it partially tucks in its wings to reduce wind resistance until it is close enough to the prey to strike. The peregrine dive, or "stoop," is so powerful that the impact can break the back of the prey. Then the peregrine circles back and grabs the spoils. Prey the size of blue jays or smaller are simply

PEREGRINE FALCON: FASTEST SKYDIVER, AT REST AND IN A DIVE

plucked from the air. Skilled at maneuvering, peregrines sometimes devour their prey while "on the wing."

Like all raptors, or birds of prey, peregrines have extremely acute vision with which they locate their prey. But the pointed wings of falcons are what make them such powerful speedsters of the sky, able to outfly all other birds except swifts. Though peregrines are the fastest, the same basic wing shape is seen in all the falcons. From the larger gyrfalcon of the Arctic, to the smaller merlins and kestrels of our fields and forests, falcons are built for speed and maneuverability.

VULTURE: SHARP-SIGHTED BIRD OF PREY

ANIMAL WEIGHT LIFTERS

The elephant is the strongest land animal in the world, able to lift hundreds of pounds in the air with its trunk. But, believe it or not, ounce for ounce, the lowly ant earns the weight-lifting trophy. Some ants, of which there may be 12,000 to 14,000 species, can lift an object up to fifty times their body weight and carry it around over their heads. And they don't do this with their feet, but with their mouths! Through cooperative behavior they are able to accomplish even more. You may have seen a small group of a dozen or so ants dragging along a comparatively gigantic grasshopper which, in fact, could weigh a thousand times as much as one of the tiny worker ants.

Scientists estimate that over 10 percent of all the living things on earth at any given time are ants. Many ant colonies contain over a million individual ants, and some tropical army ants form gigantic colonies with up to twenty million workers under one "roof."

Among the strongest of the weight-lifting ants are the leaf-cutting ants of the genus *Atta*, from Central and South America. They are named leaf-cutters or leaf-cutting because they forage

LEAF-CUTTING ANTS: CHAMPION WEIGHT-LIFTERS

in trees, using their sharp pincers to cut off big sections of leaves and carry them to the nest. One species carries such huge leaves above its head that it is called the parasol ant.

Interestingly, the leaf-cutters do not eat the leaves. They couldn't digest them. In fact, they eat only a certain species of fungus. All the work of carrying leaves back to the nest is to provide food to grow the fungi, which they use to make their underground nests, as well as their dinners. You could say they invented farming.

These two species, ants and fungi, are so dependent upon one another that neither can exist without the other. If a colony becomes overpopulated, the queen ant produces a new queen, complete with wings, who flies off and establishes a new nest. But in order for the future colony to survive, the new queen must take along a small quantity of the fungus to begin a "farm."

THE INSECT-EATING CHAMPIONS

Most of the bats of the world eat insects for their late-night snacks. And, contrary to many legends, they are our friends; just one bat can consume 700 pesky mosquitoes in a single evening. In the American Southwest a single cave can serve as home to a colony of bats, which will fly out and devour a quarter of a million pounds (over 113,000 kg) of insects every night!

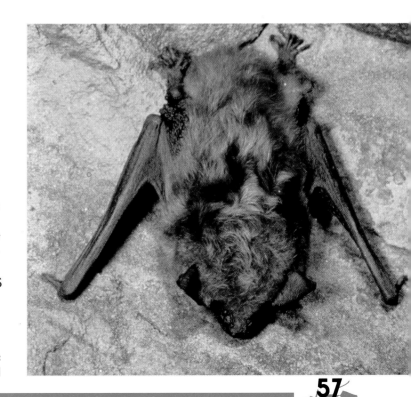

BROWN BAT:
AN INSECT-EATING CHAMPION

In many parts of the world people eat insects too. That may sound surprising, but remember, what we think of as a treat may seem awful to people in other regions. For example, our old standby, peanut butter and jelly, is detested by people in parts of Asia. But in rural markets throughout Indonesia you can sometimes find water bugs for sale as a food item. In remote villages throughout the tropics you may find insects on the menu. A popular food in South America is the Hercules beetle, one of the largest of all insects. The adult beetles, with their hard exoskeletons and the huge pincers on the male, would be too difficult to eat. But, as beetle larvae living underground, they are a delicacy in the making. The giant grubs are 5 to 6 inches (13–15 cm) in length and about 1 inch (2.5 cm) in diameter. When cooked they look like a big white sausage or the bratwurst you can buy at a baseball game in some areas of our country. We may turn our noses up at the thought of eating these giant grubs, but the joke is on us. Insect larvae is a health food, natural and rich in protein, while hot dogs and brats are filled with animal fats, nitrites and nitrates—all things that nutritionists advise us to avoid.

A HERCULES BEETLE
AND ITS GIANT GRUB

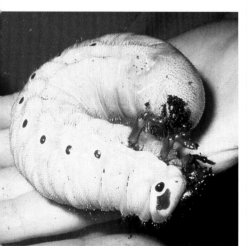

MOLE: AN INSECTIVORE

Birds, fish, frogs, and bats (and people) aren't the only eaters of insects. In fact, there is an entire order of mammals called the insectivores, or insect-eaters, which includes a variety of voracious feeders, from moles and shrews to hedgehogs. Insects make up 100 percent of the diet of all insectivores. But don't worry, there will still be plenty of bugs when springtime comes again, because not even West Texas bats can eat them all.

SOARING TO OLYMPIC HEIGHTS

Birds that fly the highest and the farthest are built so they can do so with the least amount of effort. They are top-notch energy conservationists. In fact, some are so good at flying that they seem hardly to beat their wings at all. Hawks and vultures that soar over land, and their seagoing cousins such as the albatross and the frigate bird, can fly long distances with the least altitude loss and wing flapping of all birds.

Birds that soar over land have wings designed to catch moving wind or a **thermal**, that is, a rising body of warm air. As the earth warms up from the heat of the sun, hot air rises from the ground in the form of a giant bubble to form the thermal. The birds use their big, broad wings to catch updrafts from the thermals. Their large wing surface allows them to get maximum lift from the rising air. That's the reason that you will see hawks and vultures soaring in the country. They can circle for hours, flying from one thermal to the next. They are built for a life aloft, floating in the sky as they scan the land below for food—a task that takes most of the day.

The Andean condor, the largest cousin of the vulture, has the greatest wing surface of all birds and a wingspan of nearly 11 feet (3.4 m). Its habitat in the region of the Andes Mountains of South America offers perfect soaring conditions for these mammoth birds that can reach a weight of 25 pounds (11 kg).

AN ANDEAN CONDOR AT REST

At sea there are few thermals, so soaring seabirds like the albatross are designed to sail on the wind. Their wings are long and skinny. The albatross, frigate bird, pelican, and others use their wings to catch the wind and ride it for hours. And if you've ever been to the ocean and wondered how pelicans could glide along just above the waves without beating a wing, it is because they are *slope soaring*. As the wind blows, it rises up along the crest of the waves. The pelicans take advantage of this rising wind, which allows them to cruise along while searching the water for fish. As one wave breaks, they beat their wings just a few times, "catch" another wave, and continue their slope soaring. This is true windsurfing, isn't it?

PELICAN: SLOPE-SOARING SEABIRD

GLOSSARY

Embryo—an animal in the first stages of growth before birth

Endangered species—a group of animals or plants whose numbers are so small that it is at risk of disappearing from the Earth

Entomologist—a scientist who studies insects

Extinct—no longer in existence, having disappeared from the Earth

Fetus—an animal not yet born or hatched; more developed than an embryo

Gestation period—pregnancy; the time between conception and birth, when the young are developing

Habitat—the area and physical conditions where an animal or plant species usually lives in the wild

Hibernate—to spend the winter in a torpid, or resting, state

Locomotion—the act or method by which an animal moves from place to place

Longevity—length of life

Mammary glands—a female mammal's milk-producing glands

Marsupials—an order of mammals in which the females have a pouch on the abdomen for carrying their young; marsupials include kangaroos and opossums

Metabolism—the body processes by which a living being uses food to provide energy, build tissues, and dispose of waste

Metabolize—to take in and process food for use in the living body

Metamorphosis—a change, or transformation; in many invertebrate species, the development through stages from egg to adult

Migration—the annual movement of a species from one region to another due to changes in the climate and the food supply

Porous—having pores, or tiny holes, through which air or water may pass

Reproduce—to produce offspring

Thermal—a rising bubble of warm air, on which hawks and vultures can soar

Turbulence—irregular up-and-down air currents

Vector—an organism, such as an insect, that may serve as a carrier for disease germs

Venomous—poisonous

FURTHER READING

Benyus, Janine. *Beastly Behaviors: A Watcher's Guide to How Animals Act and Why.* New York: Addison-Wesley Publishing Company, 1992.

Burton, Robert. *Bird Flight: An Illustrated Study of Birds' Aerial Mastery.* New York: Facts on File, 1990.

Dennis, Jerry. *It's Raining Frogs and Fishes: Four Seasons of Natural Phenomena and Oddities of the Sky.* New York: Harper Collins Publishers, 1992.

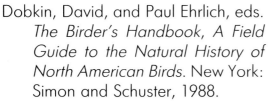

Dobkin, David, and Paul Ehrlich, eds. *The Birder's Handbook, A Field Guide to the Natural History of North American Birds.* New York: Simon and Schuster, 1988.

Downer, John. *Supersense: Perception in the Animal World.* New York: Henry Holt and Company, 1988.

Fenton, Brock. *Bats.* New York: Facts on File, 1992.

Hansen, Jeanne. *Of Kinkajous, Capybaras, Horned Beetles and Seladangs, and the Oddest and Most Wonderful Mammals, Insects, Birds and Plants in Our World.* New York: Harper Collins Publishers, 1991.

McWhirter, Norris, ed. *The Guiness Book of Olympic Records.* New York: Bantam Books, 1992.

Pope, Joyce. *Do Animals Dream?* London: Viking Kestrel Publishing, 1986.

Rees, Robin. *The Way Nature Works.* New York: Macmillan Publishing Company, 1992.

Scheffel, Richard, ed. *ABC's of Nature.* New York: Reader's Digest Books, 1984.

Whitfield, Philip. *Can the Whales Be Saved?* London: Viking Kestrel Publishing, 1989.

Wood, Gerald. *Guiness Book of World Records: Animal Facts and Feats.* New York: Bantam Books, 1978.

Periodicals

Audubon magazine

International Wildlife magazine

National Wildlife magazine

NatureScope, National Wildlife Federation, 1412 16th Street, NW, Washington, DC 20036-2266

Wildlife Conservation magazine

ZOOBOOKS, 930 W. Washington Street, San Diego, California 92103

INDEX

Italicized page numbers refer to illustrations.

Aardvarks, 24–26, *25*
Albatross, 59, 61
Alligators, *43*
Antelope, 30, *30*
Ants, 56–57
Archerfish, 32, *32*
Arctic tern, 33–34, *34*

Bacteria, 9, *9*
Bats, 16, *16, 42*, 57, 59
Bears, 9, 12, 30, 50
Beetles, 22, *23*, 53, 58
Blue jays, 41, 54
Butterflies, 17–19, *17, 18, 19*, 53

Camels, 10–11, *11*
Cardinals, 34–35
Cats, 19, 30, *30*
Cheetahs, 29, *29*
Chickens, 31
Cicadas, 10, *10*
Cobras, 33, *33*
Crocodiles, 9, 12

Deer, 30
Dogs, 19, 24

Dragonflies, 53
Duck-billed platypus, 13

Elephants, *8, 9,* 13, *14,* 31, 41, 47, 56
Endangered species, 27, 62
Entomologists, 18, 62
Extinction, 36, 62

Fetus, 29, 62
Fish, 32, 59
Fleas, 19–21, *20*
Flies, 9, 53
Frigate birds, 59, 61
Frogs, 20, *21,* 23, 42, 59

Gestation periods, 13, *14, 15,* 62
Giraffes, 15–16, *15*
Gorillas, 48
Groundhogs, 51

Habitat, 27, 62
Hawks, 59–60
Hedgehogs, 51, 59
Herbivores, 13
Hibernation, 23, 50–51, 62
Humans, 9, 13, 37, 41, 47, 50, 58, 59
Hummingbirds, 39–41, *40,* 48, 52

Kangaroos, 13, 27, 28, *28*
Kestrels, 55
Koalas, 13

Ladybugs, 53
Lions, 20, 24, 30

Mammals, 13, 29, 59
Mammary glands, 46, 62
Marmot, 51
Marsupials, 13, 27, 62
Martens, 31
Merlins, 55

Migration, 17, 33–35
Moles, 59
Mosquitos, 12–13, *12,* 53, 57

Opossum, 13–15, *15*
Ostrich, 42, *43,* 48

Parrots, 48, *49*
Pelicans, 61
Penguins, 37, *38*
Peregrine falcons, 44, *44,* 54–55

Rabbits, 9, 20, 31
Reproduction, 9, 12–15, 16, 20, 29, 62

Sailfish, 38–39, *39*
Sea anemones, 48, *49*
Sea lions, 35
Seals, 35, 37
Sharks, 12, 35–36, *36*
Shrews, 48, 59
Snails, 31, *31*
Snakes, 31, 33
Starfish, 22, *24*
Swifts, 44–45, *45*

Termites, 25, *25, 26*
Tortoise, 31, 47, *48*
Tuna, 37, *37*
Turbulence, 52, 62
Turtles, 9, 23

Vectors, 12, 62
Vultures, 59–60

Walruses, 21, *22*
Water bugs, 58
Whales, 13, *14,* 21, *22,* 35, *36,* 46, *46,* 47, 48
Wolves, 9, 41, *42*